Second Tongue

ALSO BY JUDITH SMALL

From the Island

Second Tongue

Poems

by

Judith Small

BRIGHT
HORSE
BOOKS

Brighthorse Books
13202 North River Drive
Omaha, NE 68112

ISBN: 978-1-944467-12-8

Author Photo © Nabor Godoy
Cover Art © Rachell Sumpter

For permission to reproduce selections from this book and for more in-
formation about Brighthorse Books and the Brighthorse Book Awards,
visit us on the web at brighthorsebooks.com.

Brighthorse books are distributed to the trade through Ingram Book
Group and its distribution partners.

These poems have grown out of my work in San Francisco as an interpreter, translator, and paralegal for French-speaking asylum seekers from North and West Africa, referred for pro bono representation by the Lawyers' Committee for Civil Rights of the San Francisco Bay Area and Human Rights First. The poems also draw on interviews and observations I conducted in Houston and Galveston, in 2007, with unaccompanied minors in immigration custody, their caregivers and teachers, as part of a study by the Women's Refugee Commission in collaboration with the law firm of Orrick, Herrington & Sutcliffe LLP. I have changed all names and identifying details of the individuals whose stories I tell.

For each of those seeking asylum
whose lives I have been honored to share;

in memory of
Joan Kramer, Eve Dearborn, and Dinah Bromberg,
camarades de classe perdues trop tôt;

and for Bob

Contents

Stories come to us like new senses.
—W.S. Merwin

Hibou

1.

I had just turned eleven when I chose
my name,

had just started French and didn't know
much
    barely knew
        beaucoup
            had trouble remembering so long
            a story,
                all those vowels-in-a-row for no
                good reason
                        when one
                        would have done
            not to mention that *p*
            silent, mysterious
                glistening
                        like slipping
        out on the morning's freshly-waxed
        linoleum, all the way down the long hall to the
        bathroom without a pass.

I was the only one.
All the other girls knew everything,
                each other and
all the words.

My parents wanted the best for me, thought this
private school would be better.

What could they know of the
slippery, half-lit corridor

of all I didn't know?

2.

When a girl named Claudia, some forty
years later, forded the Rio Grande,

she knew
to be careful.

Of course she had to watch the coyote up ahead. Everybody
knew that.

Of course she had to watch for *La Migra*. Everybody,
even the *más tonto*, everybody
knew that.

But there was something else only
she knew

and folded it many times over

and pressed it deep down
to the bottom of the deepest pocket of her jeans

so that all the numbers would be there for her
in their neat line of blue

waiting
till she reached the other side

just as Papá had written them

on the page he tore from her assignment pad

waiting
so she could call her uncle Raúl, her aunt Susana,
her cousin Julieta who Papá said was close to her age

if only she had known
the mighty waters

how they seep and blur

how they wash away what is blue and sure
and given

and gone.

3.

hibou (pl. hiboux)
/ibu/ (n.m.) owl

Hibou
was the name I wanted when Madame Hill
asked us each to choose.

Now we would no longer be known
in the old way

as when in a prior life someone called me *Judy*, called *Jude*
my head would turn

now it would move only
at the brush of a wing
a commotion in the darkest corner of the barn
two glowing eyes that knew me

a voice that called

ee-boo I said
as a small child names
a ghost
in fear and delight

I didn't care what everybody thought
didn't want *Jacqueline*
didn't want *Emilie*

knew only that I loved
French sounds, how they took

my lips
my tongue
my throat

trembling at times like a mouse
between talons

but other times riding
the wingspan, clutching
the feathers knuckle-deep

over the churning waters

4.

In class we sat down for breakfast with
Monsieur and Madame Vincent.

Also, their two well-mannered children,
Pierre and Josette.

Nobody ate a thing.
This wasn't that kind of breakfast.

Instead, turning pages to the morning's
dialogue, Madame Hill would guide us through
the intricate dance,

teaching us each to step gracefully between
le and *du*,

between definite and partitive
articles

le sucre: sugar-in-general, barely
a bubble in God's brain the morning before
creation

du sucre: sugar-right-here
on this carefully-laid table,

in a bowl hand-painted with
small flowers, mustard and blue

as Monsieur and Madame presided over
spoons, *petites et grandes.*

Bonjour said Monsieur
Bonjour said Madame

and Pierre
and Josette,
likewise

welcoming the new initiates

each of us with our bowl
of coffee and warm milk,
our bread

our place at the table

5.

How could I not have seen
what was clear and right

before my eyes   bright star
in my cloudy patch of sky?

Ellen's test paper
smooth under her broad hand

looping steadily, surely
each *o* and *a* and *l*
across the lozenge-shaped desk

without pause because
Ellen (Hélène) knew everything

and had a name that crossed
the border
without incident.

I sat
behind,
bewildered in this new place

knowing only that I longed
again to be the girl who was always

straight-A right.

So when I looked
up, by chance, from the
desk where I labored and saw

the word I had forgotten
shiny round and ripe

on Ellen's paper not so very
far up ahead
                    I reached
out, I plucked
the apple
            la pomme
                    so now
I would have one too

and dropped it
into
my empty basket

without a sound.

6.

That night, when my mother
sat at the edge of my bed

between dark and darker
between *bon soir* and *bonne nuit,*

(good evening, good night) something

softened slightly
on the bed between us

as if a snake coiled tight to strike had instead
slipped away, easing

its sinuous length
through grass
              or as if the grass itself
knew the way
and bowed down

to where my story lay
to where I could no longer lie

and my mother, before she bent
her head to kiss me,
              told me
to talk to Madame Hill

and Madame Hill, because

I had come forward of my own

accord, took off
the points I had won

with Ellen's word,
and nothing more,
                           and turned
to adjust her grade book,

her blue pen poised
above the numbers
in their crowded rows

the classroom quiet

the other girls had rushed off
clattering to math

I would be late

with my empty basket
                           adrift in my small boat

I must find my way.

Aissata

SALL, Aissata
Alien #_____
b. Nzerekoré, Republic of Guinea, 3/5/1963
Married, two biological children, two adopted

Left Conakry, Guinea 8/11/2004 with son Boubacar, aged
17; arrived New York, 8/12/2004, on connecting flight from
Morocco.

Application for asylum based on political persecution by
government of General Lansana Conté due to membership in
political party opposing, among other governmental actions,
constitutional amendment granting to Conté the right to run
indefinitely for re-election.

1.

Still dark when they woke her, maybe
six. She was maybe
seven.

Her father's sister's
hand on her shoulder
didn't hurt. But Auntie Hawa said
she had to come. They walked

in darkness
through the village. There were other
women she thought she
knew.

But not
the house—she had never
seen it, didn't know

the woman who opened the door

who set her
down on a low chair

who tied her eyes
tight shut

but just before
the woman pulled the soft
cloth snug, Aissata

saw, near the woman's hand, a small
bright knife with a little

handle, tied with a fuzzy piece
of red string.

After, she pressed
her legs together hard. The woman

gave her clean, fresh
clothes now
her life was new.

So at home, after weeks of rubbing with
herbs and shea butter, after weeks of missing

school as she waited for
the burning to leave her body, everyone

was ready
to eat and dance—

all the uncles, aunts, cousins, all the
brothers and sisters and neighbors—the ones they
liked a lot, sure, but even

the guy who said she was too young to try his
wobbly, rusted-out bike

and her father
and her mother

everybody

dancing in a blaze
of laughter and guitars.

But she knew
from now on

she must move more
carefully through the world

holding
always in her eyes

from that last moment
before the dark

in the deepest
folds and turnings of her body

so small a knife and
string so red.

2.

Conakry, Guinea, 2001

Four *gendarmes* showed up that night.

Aissata was eating dinner with her
husband, their children, her younger
brother, her husband's nephew.

Aissata didn't remember inviting
four *gendarmes*,
especially not *gendarmes* with
such bad manners

who kicked down the door
who screamed her name
who screamed her husband's name
Abdoul, Abdoul

and all the while,
outside, the van
          (but it's so much prettier in French, *n'est-ce pas?*
                  la camionnette)

waited in the dark
to receive them
          (if you didn't know better you might think
          oh, *la*

camionnette,
might imagine one of Degas' tired
dancers on break,
limbs folded over like the wings of a
lark, *une alouette*)

the *camionnette*
had a seat for her, and a seat
for Abdoul as well

the *camionnette*
stopped here, stopped there

the *gendarmes*
stepped out and delivered their
pressing invitations

one for each of Aissata's friends,
and for Abdoul's as well

for everyone who had ever
sat in the house talking late into the night, drinking
cup after cup of mint tea

but when the *camionnette* pulled up to the prison
something had gone wrong

so close to the President's palace but here
one cell for ten people, men and women
crammed together like
toes in a too-tight shoe

no tea for them, nor bread

nor could she relieve herself
decently, in her customary way

in one corner of the cell, a hole

How could the President and all his *gendarmes*
confuse a hole with a
toilette?

•   •   •

In the morning, the officers
commenced their visits.

They took Abdoul,
and when they brought him
back, she could see

all over his body
his answers had not pleased them.

How would her words suffice when her husband's
had not?

By early evening, in another room,
one of the officers had prepared for her:

a whip

a towel, moistened to hide the signs

a book with her name in it

When Allah, in His wisdom, turns
the pages of the Book of Sorrows,

does He trace with His finger
each letter of her name?

3.

Fearing for her safety in a neighborhood
dominated by supporters of President Conté,
Applicant was forced to disguise herself in long
black robes.

In darkness, before daybreak, she left the house

In darkness she returned, shrouded
always in her cloak of shadows

She who had wanted simply
to walk by day
into the marketplace

to greet without haste each
friend in their several tongues

to banter, to bargain, to
bluff and feint

there among the carrots and peanuts,
the onions piled high,

the marketwomen bright with
lemons and shouts

but when the soldiers came again

for Abdoul,

the sun went down all
over her life.

That afternoon she was at work while
Abdoul, in the courtyard,

sat with Boubacar after school,
heads bent over a

math problem Boubacar had asked for
help with

Suddenly the book slammed shut.

The soldiers wanted Boubacar to solve
a few different problems:

If one man and one boy are dragged to prison, how many blows
can each one bear?

How many millions of Guinean francs must one woman pay
so that one guard will take one five-minute break at precisely
the right time?

And:

Brain-teaser/Extra credit

If the lives of one man and one boy are worth (see above) x

million Guinean francs,

how can it be that, three days after x million francs are paid,

only the boy
comes home?

Conduit

*The interpreter as a neutral conduit interprets
everything that is said, adding nothing,
omitting nothing, and changing nothing.
[...] **Conduit** is the role on which interpreters
should fall back if there is any uncertainty
about which role they should play.*

(From "Roles of an Interpreter," Language
Access Project, Community Legal Services,
Inc.)

The second time I interpreted for Aissata,
she wanted to know:

Is my attorney competent?
How could he have made this mistake?

I knew
it wasn't the attorney but the
judge's clerk who had made the mistake,

the mistake that meant Aissata's hearing would be delayed
six months.

I repeated Aissata's questions.
I repeated the attorney's answers.

I kept myself
invisible.

The fourth time I interpreted for Aissata,
she wanted to know:

How can this be happening? How is it that Boubacar is telling
    me
only now, two days before the hearing,
that he and his buddies had a run-in last month
with the police, who could get him sent back
to Guinea?

I repeated Aissata's questions.
I repeated the attorney's answers.

I kept myself
transparent.

Half a year later, after
her case has been won, Aissata and I
have coffee. She tells me

a secret, pressing
on my mind like a nose against glass.

The secret has nothing
to do with her case.

I keep it.

I keep it here.

Consecutive

For the first time the attorney asks her, in our final practice before the hearing, "Where do you think your husband is now?"

"He's dead," we expect her to say quickly, Aissata the strong, the clear-eyed. Instead she hesitates, then says finally, "I don't know"—her voice breaking—"sometimes I console myself by thinking, maybe he's in the Maison Centrale [the largest prison, in Conakry], but other times I think, *non, c'est pas possible*, it's not possible—that blow to the head—he's dead."

•   •   •

He is
     where no one knows
where he is
    où il se trouve

Il est où, votre mari?

     Your husband, where
     is he, could he

     possibly
     be

     anything other than
     not?

Aissata's voice then

my voice
              her
voice then my
voice following

Parfois je me console
Sometimes I
console myself

                        "consecutive
interpreting" the manual
calls it I

call it
finding a path

              We each
live elsewhere
but not

at this moment we
tell

a single
story

              C'est pas
possible   It's not
possible

              and yet

each of us

a deer

                  stepping
carefully through woods,
sounding the half-dark

ears alert,
nostrils open

breathing what may come
                          she

pauses I
pause
      she

bows I
bow

our heads bending
low

drink from the same
water

flowing

Sedira

BERKANI, Sedira
Alien Registration #_____
b. Staoueli, People's Democratic Republic of Algeria, 11/6/1952
Divorced, three children

Left Algiers, Algeria, 12/11/2006; arrived San Francisco
12/12/2006.

Application for asylum based on membership in particular social
group of formerly-married women who are unable to leave
long-term abusive relationships. Applicant claims that Algerian
government has been unable or unwilling to control actions of
ex-husband, an Islamic fundamentalist and former police officer,
whose alleged violence has been inspired in part by Applicant's
rise during the course of their marriage, after two years of post-
secondary training as an accountant, to become one of the few
women employed at the upper levels of the Algerian taxing
authority.

1.

Il était une fois

                    Once upon a time

there was a little girl whose mother
didn't speak.

Plus précisément

                    More precisely,

she spoke to the little girl's
five brothers and four sisters,

but when the mother was angry,
                    she didn't
speak to the little girl.

Each time her parents had
words with each other,
             each
shout, each bashed-in door

the mother saw, or thought
she saw, how the

girl, by glance, by furtive
touch, offered to her father
solace.

So the mother stretched her silence four
months   five months   six

like a long-legged traveler lazing out his
bones before a hearth in winter

the silence
settled in.

2.

Alors, dès sa petite enfance

So, from her early childhood

Sedira needed
an interpreter

sister speaker go-
between
bearer of the mother's
messages:

Siham, three years older,
calling
Sedira in,
"Stop
playing it's time for supper!"

as Sedira waited
still
outside in the falling dark

immersed in mid-
game of *cache-cache* (hide and seek)

hearing, from where she crouched
in her secret place,

the numbers called out fast

un
deux
trois
quatre

ready or not here I come!

each number with its name so

clear
pulsing
sturdy

as her heart

3. Audition

San Francisco 2007

*Applicants testifying before asylum officers
in a language other than English are
responsible for providing their own
interpreters. Members of the applicant's family
are discouraged from serving in this role
in order to ensure that the applicant is not
inhibited from speaking truthfully by family
ties or sensitivities.*

She wanted to see,
said Sedira's sister—fluent in Arabic,
French and English—if I was
the real thing.

Neither native speaker nor
pro, I have often
wondered myself—

uncertain   in this great
night forest of
words
                    where to

turn, how to
hear—among the variant

calls signaling
food or *love* or *home*

                pulsing through

the branches of the dense
overstory—
            how to hear that sole
particular human voice,
                and then

how to speak it with my
own imperfect
tongue.

"Who who" says the owl in English.
Hou-hou says *hibou* in French.

Neither language lifts
one feather of

the real bird

looming, massive
above

as if all the darkness
of one cold night over
one swift-flowing river

gathered itself
and hung

over the quicksilver
fish

in that split-instant un-
touched by any language

before the wings
beat once
again and the talons

take hold

.   .   .

Because time is running
out, the sister and I will talk

by phone, an audition
I prepare for with the non-native's

excruciating care. I'm about
to leave the country for a week, to step

on a plane the next day and fly over
water, fathoms deep,
                              and over
borders, to skirt
for the moment their invisible
zipper teeth.

She will want to know

where I come from, how I know
what I know.

As I pick up the phone, I'm
already heading into

uncertain weather, possible
turbulence, occasional atmospheric
pressure.

I want to show her that at least
I know my way around
the subjunctive—
                                    always good for points—
that sacrifice offered

up to the world by every
Romance language to acknowledge

hesitation, doubt, the press
of emotion, of
                        what is needed, what we

desire
or long for.

I want her to know
                        Je veux qu'elle sache

that I want to know
her sister

that I will do my best
to speak for Sedira

autant que ce soit possible

                              to the extent this is,
or may be, possible.

And suddenly, with my words, the sister
shifts
into English, wants

to find out when I'll return from my trip so
Sedira and I can meet

as if the sister

knows
for the moment

all she wants
all she needs

4.

How could she
have known, before

the wedding, who he
was or would

become? Sedira
knew only

her parents' house, or
classrooms where she finished

each of the weekly quizzes
early, and sat

hands folded, desk
clear, her mind

racing ahead to meet some other,
brighter life.

Even when she started
working,
          heading

out with each new
project as if mounted

on her own

strong horse,
                    sensing

the numbers massed
behind her like

cavalry, column
after column, the early

sun catching the
glint of their

flanks like
steel, like truth

                    —even then she needed
someone to flee with,

to escort her inconspicuously past
the roadblocks everywhere set for

a woman alone.

Kamel seemed
nice, he seemed—

in the company of friends or family (almost
never were they only

two)—as if he could be
the one

who would turn to her
after the wedding

in their own
new place and speak

softly, there would be
someone singing

on the radio   Kamel would
know

to take his
sweet time with

her
to go

slowly
slowly

5.

Not once did she ever
say yes

J'ai pas accepté
                    I didn't accept

Certainly not
that first time

when he wanted it
all

right now
                when he chose

the hardest
way in

so he could
know for sure,

he told her,
           she had

never
before

been touched

6. Portrait of a Marriage in Aerial Objects

Objects thrown
        through the air
                during the

numerous years of their
           marriage included
                  the usual

household items
        (dinner plates, chairs)
                but also

a bucketful of water
         tossed
              over Sedira's head

by a policeman
         manning the night desk
                who wanted

her to calm down
        (*calme-toi, calme-toi*)
              when she tried

to file a complaint.

At times the home air
        positively hummed with
              threats, fuzzy and fat

as flies,
        dive-bombing the kitchen
                greedy for honey-cakes,
                        cooling by the stove.

"If you do not…" they buzzed
                (have sex with me,
                    quit your job,
                        stop listening to pop music)
"then I will…"
              they vroomed
                    they revved:
slice your throat
with my Swiss Army knife

on the tile where I
slaughter the lamb at Eid I will

cut off your head

and if, by some
dark magic you

escape
and live,

at night I will send a
devil in the form of a

little worm

who will sneak into
your mind

who will nibble it
clean away

7.

Algerian law permits divorce only if the husband agrees or has been convicted of a serious crime. During her twenty-seven years of marriage, and beginning in the first year, Applicant filed four divorce requests with the Algerian courts; all were denied. After one request Applicant was ordered by the court to return home and not leave without her husband's permission.

J'ai failli perdre la raison

                  I almost went crazy

Instead, her children
circled her

like shields, mounded
high, nested

around their mother they
kept vigil even

as they slept.

They knew he wouldn't
touch them but he

got to her
anyway:

once
he looked down, his

hands held
hair, a strip of
scalp

That time she'd pulled
away but
                another

time his knife
pushed deep

Sometimes she'd sleep
at the office

Sometimes when she
disagreed with her boss she spoke

her mind

Tu te bagarres avec les hommes maintenant?
her husband asked,
                You're getting in fights with men now?

He wondered what people would say

So one day
Sedira
played Kamel

a trick

(*Je lui ai joué une astuce*)

his brother wasn't
a bad guy
            so she

invited him over

made sure he was
listening when she told
Kamel:

a man who says
no when his

wife asks for a
divorce
is not

a man.

I'm your wife, she said,
I'm asking

again.

And because his brother
was listening
this time
Kamel

couldn't
say no

in his brother's eyes
he had to be

the man
who let her

go

8.

*Applicant contends that attacks by her ex-
husband intensified after the divorce because he
was unable to accept it. As the divorce decree
left title to the family home in the name of both
Applicant and her ex-husband, she was forced
to continue living in the house, which her ex-
husband refused to sell. Applicant installed
locks on her bedroom and constructed a side
entrance, but found herself vulnerable in shared
areas such as kitchen and bathroom.*

While the house was split
in two,

Sedira also lived
in halves.

In one half—her children grown, her sister
living in the US—
                    Sedira planned
her flight.

In the other half, she kept
a promise:
            that when her father was dying

she would be there
to care for him.

He was leaving now, and so,
for now,
Sedira would stay.

Years later she would still believe
in his last breaths

he had sung
two songs for her:

Adieu was one,
adieu

and the second,
Bon voyage

9. Epilogue

Applicant granted asylum March 12, 2008,
subsequent to interview at San Francisco
Asylum Office. Permanent resident status
granted July 18, 2009; citizenship granted
July 30, 2013.

In the course of her work, she had come upon
some who owed but hadn't
paid.

She made sure that her cause was
just, but once she knew,
she swooped.

That flashy car at the curb?
No more worries about making it shine.

That necklace you brought back from Paris to surprise
your expensive girlfriend?
Sorry, pal, *au revoir.*

Oh and that sweet little villa where you like to
meet her, just outside of town?

                               (nothing too
pretentious, couple of fig trees,

                                      nice
terrace to catch the breeze)

                            Enjoy it
while you can,

the lien

in time will work
its magic.

Sedira could be somewhere
else, even in

some other country

when you go to bed, the villa's
yours but when the sun
comes up,
                voilà:

Suddenly your private nest
turns into

la maison du peuple
                the people's house.

·   ·   ·

In my house we like to tell a story about my late mother-in-law, Sophie Fitzgerald. Sophie was a fearless and effective union organizer who was frequently fired once her employers figured out what she was up to. So it happened that, during the thirties, one afternoon in downtown Paterson, New Jersey, Sophie had just been fired from her job as a retail clerk at Meyer Brothers' Department Store.

Before she said her last farewell, though, Sophie paid a visit to the Housewares Department, where she secretly, systematically set each alarm clock on the floor to go off precisely thirty minutes after she definitively left the premises. Let's say she walked out at 2:30. At 3:00, then, let's imagine every alarm clock in the store starting to ring hard and high, starting to clang, starting to rattle, as each clock in its distinctive voice took its brief but delicious revenge.

Of course Sedira's leaving was different. But like Sophie, she seeded the site of her apparent defeat with an invisible trail of time-release capsules, each primed to deliver its message at the appropriate time. Even now, somewhere in Algeria, an alarm could be ringing, a lien could be sinking its teeth. Something could be shifting. Something could vanish, something could stay.

10. For Sedira, My Song

He can knock all day and into the night
(Big devil, little worm)

Front door's flapping
Side door too

Up and away
My words for you

Désolée
        So terribly sorry

Monsieur le Diable
          You devil you

ain't nobody

home

Birahim

KANTE, Birahim
Alien #_____
b. Conakry, Republic of Guinea, 3/3/1975
Single, no children

Left Conakry, Guinea 7/24/2004; arrived Montreal, Canada 7/25/2004 on connecting flight from Morocco. Arrived New York by bus, 7/26/2004. Arrived San Francisco by plane, 7/27/2004.

Application for asylum based on membership in particular social group of homosexual men.

1.

*One of five brothers, Applicant spent his
childhood and early adulthood in a village
where his father served as the imam. In
order to exemplify for his community the
strict obedience required by his exacting
interpretation of Islam, Applicant's father
disciplined his children regularly and in public.*

He who called a village to prayer five times a day
called his sons each week
to account:

For Samba's two eyelids, fluttering
their way back into sleep, though Allah at first light requires
otherwise, even from the youngest of
these His servants.

For each of Diogo's ten miscreant
toes—wriggling, stubbed, unclean—sneaking
away from the family compound whenever there were
chores to be done, or a neighbor to be summoned,
should the imam have need.

And how can it be that two
pairs of ears, pasted by their Maker one on each side of
two small, thick skulls—of Abdourahamane, of his twin
    Abdellatif—

how can four ears be too few to attend
to a father's righteous words?

But gravest of all was the trespass
of Birahim's two legs, two arms and two unseeing eyes,
that pedaled the wheels, that gripped the handlebars, that failed
    to detect
the rock in the road that bent the frame
of the bicycle, the blue bicycle
lent by the father with a trusting heart to his
feckless son.

For these transgressions a man must require
a high price.

From among the faithful, summoned, he chose
only the four most stalwart, one
for each limb.

He bade them pin
boy to ground, then
surveyed without flinching

flesh of his flesh
below him, splayed,
crossed out.

And the father took
one stick

and did
his duty

as he saw
fit,

blow
upon blow.

2.

In high school Birahim began to notice
things the other boys missed.

When Salif—captain of the soccer team, everybody loved
Salif—when Salif

with one touch of his foot tipped
the afternoon's slow-burning, wadded-up heat into

flame, as shot upon shot
blazed its path across the

dusty pitch—when he
raised both arms as if throwing

a window wide open, welcoming
goal upon goal—Birahim

heard, beneath the shouts, what the body
whispered, faint

as eyelash drifting
onto cheekbone.

Of these soft sounds, Salif
knew nothing. Birahim knew

the other boys knew
nothing. But he was ready for

Stéphane, five years later, when he came
to town, a young engineer on his first

overseas post to a nearby
mine. They drank

tea together, cup after cup, watched
soccer, off and on, whenever

the café's TV held up. Whenever
it didn't, they

kept talking, kept on talking until they
stopped. Often,

it would be evening, they would welcome
the darkness, closing

in. Till the father's voice rang out
over the shadowy

streets, tolling the day's
last prayers.

Au revoir were words they learned to speak
in whispers.

3.

When Applicant reached his late teens, his
father began pressuring him to marry, as was
customary in the community and expected, in
particular, for the son of an imam. Applicant's
father had arranged for his son to marry
the daughter of a friend. Applicant resisted,
however, claiming he needed more time to
complete his schooling and learn a trade.

The father has a gift
for his son. He has arranged for him to be served
a special dish.

The father knows, beyond any questioning, that this
is a dish of the highest quality. For centuries now,
or much longer, to mark occasions of particular import,
the households of the village have prepared
this dish, simmering
in a fragrant broth.

"Come," the father says to his son, "sit down."
Graciously, he beckons.

He has arranged for a woman of the village known for her skills
in the arts of the feast
to mix red chiles, onions, green mangoes, white-fleshed
carp from the river, smoked
to keep its sweetness all the long
lifetime of a man.

"You must eat this," he says. "It can't wait."

The son is surprised to receive a gift
from his father, who has offered to him—
and to his brothers, and to their mother also—
only harsh words, until this day.
Until this day, only beatings.

The son is hungry beyond imagining
for warmth, for sweetness. For spice.

Yet he knows
that to eat this dish would be to devour,
as well, his heart.

To take this dish
into his body would mean for him
a long lifetime
of dying.

"Father," he says, "I cannot—
I am not—
ready," he says. "Not now."

4.

*When Applicant was in his mid-twenties,
his father—frustrated by Applicant's repeated
excuses for deferring marriage—gathered
together near the family compound, one
afternoon after Friday prayers, Applicant's
mother and brothers, the father's friend, the
friend's daughter, and a large number of
community members, some of whom were
waiting to ask the imam for counsel. For the
first time in a public forum, Applicant's father
offered marriage to his son and demanded to
know why he had refused it.*

The son has waited many years
to answer his father.

A question kept waiting so long for an answer deserves
nothing less than the truth.

The son tells his father he can never marry
the friend's daughter.

He can never marry her because
she is a woman, and he
is a man who loves only men.

The son senses, for one moment, the angel of truth
tall at his side. The angel wears a cloak of flame.
His sword is mighty, and will protect.

This is a lie.
There is no angel. Instead

there is the father, alone in the glaring sunlight
of his shame.

"You are not my son," says the father. "You are a beast
who must die."

Suddenly the faithful
turn on the imam's son

Chien de gay they shout "dog of a gay" they
spit he tries to run but they

catch him they
fall on him with

stones

under the
blows

he is
as always

nothing

there is nothing
he can

do under the
blows
        except detect

                through the volley of taunts
                   ("dog of a gay, gay bastard,
                       bastard dog of a gay")

his mother's voice
pleading

with her neighbors and friends to spare
her son's last
flicker

of life

5.

At least once a day she comes
to his bedside at the hospital, often alone,

but sometimes with her brother, Birahim's uncle, who has given
    them
shelter in Conakry. He will continue

to shelter them when her husband
sends word

that she is no longer, under the laws of man or Allah,
his wife. He has cast her out, she who gave birth

to this unclean thing, she who chose
to rescue—with the help of certain

false friends—this unseemly
son, rather than to stay at her husband's side.

At the hospital, at least once a day, she takes from a covered
    basket
something to help her son's body mend:

chicken stewed with white onions
to repair his bones,

hibiscus juice, crimson and thick, that his blood
may nourish him once again.

As he eats, eyes closed, in silence,
as her basket empties, her mind overflows.

Where will he go, she wonders,
on this harsh earth

how will he be
and with whom

6. First Meetings

Oakland, California 2009

Birahim is telling his story to the attorney.

That is, he is telling his story in French and I am trying to tell
it in English, only I'm missing easily a fifth of his words. He's
mumbling, I'm not used to his accent, he's going too fast, I have
to keep asking him to repeat, to slow down, *doucement, s'il vous
plaît, doucement.*

Now he speaks to me in baby steps, grouping his words in threes
or twos like children in preschool out for a walk, tethered. Of
course he gets tired of this, picks up speed again, I'm catching
the gist, that's all, and the gist isn't good enough, neither am I.

After, I tell the attorney I assume she'll want to find someone
else. I've known her by reputation for years, had jumped at the
chance to work together. "Oh no," she says, "it will work out.
Let's give it some time."

On the train from San Francisco, the afternoon before our
second meeting, I hold my vocabulary notebook in my lap
for my usual review. I'm doing OK (exhibit (n.), *une pièce à
conviction*, police record, *un casier judiciaire*) until it suddenly hits
me: I can't remember the word for "post office." This word is way
too basic to rate a line in my notebook. Unbelievable that I'm
struggling. Nothing comes. Then, *la Poste,* I think. Oh.
Could there be anything more bonehead simple?

Also, I realize at the first meeting I'd almost mixed up *le lendemain*, the day after, with *la veille*, the night before. Had to pause for a split second while I untangled these words. I was, what, maybe thirteen when I first learned them? In what forest are they hiding now, behind what branches, guarded by what fierce bird?

7. Small Song

La veille le lendemain
le lendemain la veille

the day next to the day
after

night upon night
falling

silent

to where
without words and

wingless

shivering,
plucked

I dwell

8.

In a country I have never seen,
a man I don't know
is singing.

In his language there is not a single
word that I understand.

Yet I find myself
listening, over and over, to this

voice, to this sole
guitar, recorded by Victor Démé

in a tiny, makeshift
studio in Burkina Faso, then

bought by my daughter in Paris and given
to me, at Christmas.

Each time he begins, he knocks
once, twice
on the side of his guitar,

as if asking permission of the music to cross over
into that country,

or like a man who, at the threshold, removes his shoes
out of deference
for where he is about to step.

In this way he begins his song,
his voice each time

unintelligible,
pulsing,
true.

9.

I learn his voice by scanning his eyes.

Face to face,
across a café table, a teapot
between us,

I catch up to his tempo
in slow sips.

Oui, I say.
I listen.

To this day I have to ask him
to repeat sometimes, but still,

little by little,
I understand more.

That we both like the singing
of Salif Keita, are both dazzled by
Lionel Messi's moves.

That we both have mothers, far away, whom we love,
but mine
I can reach in a half-day's plane ride.

In a photograph he shows me,
his mother's face
is kind but weary.
She is my age, but has lived
longer.

Once, when the attorney asked Birahim—
out of all he had undergone—what single thing seemed to him
the most painful,

Que ma mère a souffert à cause de moi, he answered,
                                    That my mother
suffered because of me.

When his cousin Josette, with whom he lives now, takes a trip
back to Guinea, he asks her to bring his mother
a gift.

He chooses carefully, and finds for her
a pair of white shoes.

How they gleam beneath the wrapping tissue,
in Josette's overstuffed suitcase.

How staunchly
they resist utility.

How his mother, Josette reports, cradles them
on her chest,

after unfolding,
slowly, the dark, soft paper.

10. Enregistrement/Recording

Oakland, California
2012

To help Birahim prepare
for his hearing, I read

his sworn declaration out loud
in French, for a CD.

This is where his story lives now,
in a disc with his name on it, shining

pale as a moon, and so skinny
that if you were to shrink it, it would fit

on a tongue. He listens to this—
his life, my voice—over and over,

as his story spends the day by his side
and strengthens him, he tells me, but also

it has adventures, makes
enemies, machines that declare themselves

incompatible and refuse
to let his story speak, no matter how

many buttons, how many keys
are repeatedly, fruitlessly jabbed.

I have another copy made. This one travels as far as
the Costco parking lot, in Richmond,

where Birahim places it,
absent-mindedly, on the roof of Josette's car

to free up his hands as he helps her
unload groceries and paper towels.

From such a journey, this copy
will never return. Yet his story

survives, regenerates, grows
legs, and accompanies

Birahim into my office the morning before
the hearing. We sit together,

without speaking, while I work at my desk, Birahim
in a chair beside me, ears swaddled

under padded headphones, one black cord
snaking the distance

between my computer and his ears.
At one o'clock he will tell his story

to the judge, who will ask questions, who may
or may not believe his answers.

A few feet from us, in my shared office,

a phone rings. Someone picks up. Someone

pulls documents from a printer. Birahim
sees nothing. He is listening

with every part of himself—eyes intent, shoulders
low beneath a loose

brown sweater, palms
cupped and open in his lap

as if to make a nest for what
he knows now, and will speak.

He bends, for a few more moments, to
the sound of his story

through the cord, his
wounded life, coursing

11. Epilogue

Applicant granted asylum March 1, 2012, by
order of the Immigration Court. Permanent
resident status granted November 18, 2013.

We would always remember the day in San Francisco that
    Birahim
was crowned king,

which was also the day he got to reign
over a brand-new country.

She must have had a lot on her mind that morning,
the clerk at the immigration office,

besides making sure that Birahim's I-94
was issued right.

Before our eyes, as we waited at the counter, she revealed
    herself
a virtuoso of mistakes,

each one painstakingly inscribed in ballpoint, in
block letters, as version after version of the same

one-page form was offered to Birahim, and
proofread, and returned

to the woman at the counter
for correction.

His date of entry into the U.S.? The year was off, if only
by one digit.

Street address? Sorry about
that slip-up on the apartment number,

she was just trying to share with us her very own sure-fire recipe
for crucial, undeliverable mail.

But these were routine errors any
timid soul could have made. What impressed us

was the bold one she saved for last:
"Country of origin: UINEA."

Tu as ton propre pays maintenant, I whispered to him, you have
your own country now,

Uinée in French, and in English,
"Uinea" rhymes with "skinny,"

C'est toi le roi d'Uinée,
Birahim 1er,

You're the King
of Uinea, Birahim the First.

Oui, c'est ça laughs His Highness and we're still
goofy later, walking
fast through the Financial District, heading

toward the train. Suddenly Birahim

runs ahead and ducks
into a doorway—for a second I'm not sure

where he is—then, half-hidden behind
a column, his face

pops out— elfin, bright, a talking
bird in a storybook forest—

and as he laughs some more it
comes to me, I don't know

how to say
"boo!" in French
     it

doesn't matter
    I know now

each to the other
    what we mean

Ahmed

FOUDIL, Ahmed
Alien #_____
b. Sétif, People's Democratic Republic of Algeria, 1/17/1962
Married, two children

Left Algiers, Algeria, 6/1/2006; arrived San Francisco, 6/2/2006.

Application for asylum based on religious and political
persecution by Jamaa Salafia Lidaawa Walk Ital (Salafia Islamic
Army for Prayer and Combat, known since 2007 as Al Qaeda
in the Islamic Maghreb) due to status as non-observant Muslim
who owned, contrary to Sharia law, a bar-restaurant that served
alcohol.

Ne me quitte pas
Il faut oublier
Tout peut s'oublier
Qui s'enfuit déjà....

Don't leave me
We have to forget
Everything can be forgotten, everything
is vanishing already....

—Jacques Brel
"Ne me quitte pas" (1959)

Prologue

Café de l'Indépendance
Sétif, Algeria, 1982

Ne me quitte pas, don't leave me, always
this is Ahmed's song, always

the song for which his pockets
give up willingly coin after coin

as the juke box plays,
as the juke box plays

again, as the owner
steps out. She needs

lemons, maybe, or else they're running out of
ice on a hot night, the guys too busy working the crush

of customers at the bar for her
to interrupt them with errands.

When she gets back, it's
Ahmed's, his song

flooding the big room, the dark
ashtrays scattered, one to a table, the coasters

tossed carelessly as discarded
lovers out into the night, which is already

moving on, has already half-
forgotten the sound of their

beautiful, whispered
names: *Martini, Cinzano, Lillet, Dubonnet.*

Only it's her song too, hers
for years before her husband died and

she bought the place, before
Ahmed became a customer, just another

young guy stopping
by with his friends after work. Now

for a few quick moments it's
alive in the air

between them—this
occasional friendship, easy

and light until
—there it is again—

the song, Brel's voice, worked
over and over by a northern

sea, salt wind on its way to
this other country, the one that lives

between them, bounded only by the lines

of this shared song, this voice that says

don't leave me
and

I know how
to make you stay.

1.

*Prior to opening a bar-restaurant
with his brother in 1997, Appli-
cant had worked since his mid-teens
in the family business, installing
draperies, carpets, and flooring.*

By the time he left school for good he was already
half gone, tearing out of class each

afternoon so his legs could catch
up sooner to where his thoughts already

lodged. Already he had just
enough reading, just enough

math to stand
shoulder to shoulder with the men hoisting

ladders in their overalls and jumpsuits, blue
as the sky. As if to touch it, he

reached up, pressed three fingers against the measuring
tape's steelhead tip, then

stretched with his other hand the ever-
expanding tape till it

touched the sash at its outer
edge and he held the whole

window in his open arms.

Already he knew enough to feed
the men what they needed, number

after number jotted
down to guide how

high how wide   how
deep
          he could tell

Karim who had known
Ali who had known
Moustapha who had known as well

Ahmed's mother of blessed memory
Ahmed's father of blessed memory
                              also

Keltoum his stepmother who
just a few weeks before she passed had set

prunes and almonds in a covered pot to simmer
slowly with the lamb

for Ahmed
youngest of them all
                    in this
way she knew
the meat would stay

a long time
tender.
     Now for as long

as he could he stayed
constant through the afternoons, tracking

down for Ali that hammer he knew he'd
left somewhere, the little one, the one that fit so

sweet in his hand or teasing
Karim about the new girlfriend,
                   or Moustapha about

the old one, and all the while holding himself
steady, braced for the sting of this new,

unexpected life—quick
slap of cologne, cheeks tingling after a fresh,

close shave. It was as if, three
parents lost, what he found was

these afternoons, how he
gave himself to the ongoing

wash of job after job, the business thriving, the work cresting in
    mighty
waves above his head like some high ceiling, undulant
in the light

or as if someone, just
as the light was fading,
                              in some other,

distant place, had mounted
a tent—spacious, wide—had

fixed it tight and sure against night and
wind, and the seeping cold,
                              and taking

note of him, outside, had bent
down, and extended the flap,

and called out to him, *Ahmed,*

inviting him in
for a glass of tea.

2. Portrait of a Courtship with Roses and Tennis Ball

Sétif, Algeria 1993

He kept thinking he wasn't ready yet, until his brothers said,
You're ready.

And then, *We have found her*, said his sisters,
and when he saw her, yes, he had to admit

it was true.

Otherwise, how could he have thought of so many
different reasons for stopping by the
shop where she cut hair?

How could he have found that single
moment in that one afternoon, that

pause between the widow venturing
out for her semi-weekly perm
                              and the working

girl heading straight from the office for a quick
wash-and-cut before the clubs?

Into that surprising
space he placed

a dozen yellow roses, luxuriantly
circled in cellophane.

Her face

colored slightly, but she found a vase
deep and wide enough to hold them

in the back cupboard near the small fridge where she
and the other girls kept their lunches.
                                        In that same

cupboard she kept, for days,
all that wasn't ready to be spoken,

not to Souad, definitely not to
Maria, not even to Fatima,
                            at least until their regular

weekend tennis match. Then she let her thoughts
ride the ball in its easy

passage through the soft air, just
warming up, half-serious, here

a lob, there a slow graze across the net's
taut surface, till it was as if

some faster music started up, as if the ball
of its own accord began to pulse and speed

between them, and she remembered how Ahmed
had turned to her, his arms

cradling the roses against his chest like a
man with his firstborn, terrified and

fierce, breathing in for one heedless moment that heady
scent of the new—
                    and as she waited,

there on the court, her body
springy and poised for whatever the air might

bring to her, she knew it was this she
wanted, now—what he'd offered, what she'd

gathered in her arms—and the day grew
warmer, and she paused, reached

down for her water, and drank deep,
then raised

her eyes to the other side and called out,
Fatima, I'm ready.

3.

He thought it was in December. Couldn't be sure but probably yes, December. He was behind the bar in the afternoon—one of those few times when things slowed down a little—when the phone rang. He didn't know the voice. It told him selling alcohol was a sin against Islam. Ordered him to stop. Click. Maybe a joke, he thought. Maybe a competitor. The place had been doing so well it was no surprise there could be somebody out there trying to hurt his business.

•   •   •

Second call, different voice. No joke. This was maybe a week, ten days later, he couldn't be sure. This one spoke in Arabic, like the first, but more hostile. It said he had disobeyed orders. Told him again to stop. Also, it said they needed him.

He kept going but this time he worried. Told only his brother, though—not his wife, didn't want to worry her—and everybody knew you couldn't tell the police, they were either on the take or too weak to do anything.

What did it mean, *they needed him*. He had customers who worked for the government, some of them pretty high up, if the voices were terrorists they could use him, *tell us when this guy walks in, tell us when that guy gets up to leave*. It wouldn't be him planting the bomb, along the road or in the car. All the same there would be blood on his hands.

•   •   •

One day this guy walked in. Nice clothes, tough face. This was
maybe a week, ten days later. Ahmed was behind the counter
again and the guy ordered a soda. *Are you Ahmed?* he asked. Then
he put an envelope on the counter, turned and walked out.

In the envelope was a letter, written by hand in Arabic with
quotations from the Koran. Ahmed had sinned against the
Koran. He had disobeyed orders. Accordingly, he was sentenced
to death.

Someone had formed each character with the utmost care. There
were strokes that leapt before his eyes like gazelles, others that
floated like boats on the sea. A few slashed the page like sabers,
heedless, not caring that they had scarred the smooth skin of his
cheeks, that they had marked him today and for all the days of
his life to come.

•   •   •

Very late, maybe one in the morning. Maybe a week later.
Ahmed was by himself, going over receipts and getting ready
to close. Samira was upstairs in the apartment, watching TV,
waiting up for him while the children slept.

Headlights, sudden and huge where no headlights had ever
shone before. SUV smashing through the restaurant door, four
men jumping out, all limbs and dark, spidery clothes.

Shooting at him once while he fled, twice while he fled upstairs and the safety door locked shut behind him, while the children slept on and on, not hearing their mother's panicked whispers, not knowing they would wake in the morning to a father who thought he was only half a man.

4.

> *Hoping that the group that had threatened*
> *his life was restricted in its operations to*
> *his native city and the surrounding area,*
> *Applicant relocated temporarily to Algiers,*
> *where he stayed with his brother-in-law*
> *and attempted to make arrangements for his*
> *family to join him.*

Où qu'il soit
     Wherever he is
          On le trouvera
             We will find him

N'importe où, partout, toujours
          Anywhere, everywhere, always

A voice on the phone asking for Ahmed
by name

       (*Où qu'il soit, on le trouvera*
          Wherever he is, we will find him)

Ahmed had
stepped out so his

brother-in-law picked up.

After that, Ahmed knew
he couldn't stay.

Je vais où maintenant?
        Where do I go now?
                Le plus loin possible
                    As far away as possible

In America
        or wherever I
                may be that isn't

here

(*N'importe où, partout, un jour*
                Anywhere, everywhere, one day)

peut-être
       maybe
          it will be

better

5. Meetings/San Francisco 2007-2009

> *Petit à petit, l'oiseau fait son nid.—*
> Little by little, the bird
> makes its nest.
>
> —French proverb, quoted
> frequently by North and West
> Africans

New case. Owner
of a bar-restaurant, somewhere

in Algeria. Al Qaeda
tried to kill him. I

walk behind, follow
him and the attorneys into

a room made all of windows, floating
above the city. We will meet

here—or in some version of
here—that we may or

may not at first recognize—over the
course of two years.
            I will come,
little by little,
to know Ahmed

more fully, a small man, like
my father and like him, sweet–

scented, quick to anger but once
tangled in love's weave,

steadfast.

.   .   .

On prend un café ensemble? he asks, after our
first meeting, do you want to have coffee together?

Leaving the office, week after
week, over years we will find

another place—noisier, ground-
level—where we drink coffee and

tell stories. Ahmed's brother's had
heart trouble for years, *ça me pèse*, Ahmed says, it weighs on
    me, you never

know at any moment what
could happen. They had a neighbor once—friend of their
    dad's—who

choked on a chicken bone one night and
hop, *voilà!* like that, he was gone.

I know, I say, you never

know. My little brother once, when we were kids in

bathing suits, in New Jersey, put a
beach towel over his head one day just to

see what it felt like and wandered
dreamily off the edge of the

swim club pool. Luckily the lifeguard
dove right in and

fished him out. Now my parents
live in Houston, I say, my father's had

a string of small strokes, my mother
takes great care of him but he's

leaving us, little by little. Sometimes it takes
a long time.
                    Sometimes we talk about

singers we both remember and still
love, Edith Piaf, of course, Jacques Brel—

"*Ne me quitte pas,*" Ahmed asks, do you
know it? Yes, I say, I've always

loved that. I know, he says, one of the
great ones, when I was

young I couldn't get it out

of my head.
                   He shows me

pictures of Samira on their wedding day, holding
roses, and of their two boys, nine and

three when he left, now
ten and four. I ask him

what they're like, how they
get along with each other and without

their dad. Samira's a great mom, he says, but it's
really hard on her.
                   I have

children too, I tell him, show him
pictures, a boy and a girl, each one

grave and incongruously tall in their
high school soccer uniforms. They're

in their twenties now, but I still carry
these pictures. *Bien sûr*

says Ahmed, of course. I

marvel at his family, I worry, I cannot imagine how I

would survive his life but somehow I
find I know

what to say.

6.

Common psychological responses [include] re-
experiencing the trauma [through] flashbacks
or intrusive memories [...], recurrent
nightmares that include elements of the
traumatic event(s) in either their original or
symbolic form [...], avoidance
and emotional numbing, difficulty falling or
staying asleep, symptoms of depression, and
changed self-concept.

(Adapted from *Examining Asylum*
Seekers, Physicians for Human Rights)

Ne me quitte pas, he asked,
don't leave me

and the memories answered,
You will never be alone.

We will be with you, all of us, at every
turn, in sickness and in

health, in turmoil and in
stillness

                    whether you are

wakeful or asleep though sleep will visit you
rarely

When you step out for one last
smoke, when your eyes

shift sideways to scan your
phone when you tear

the edge off
a packet of sugar then stir it

fast with a skinny
stick into your coffee (regular, black)
                                    We are the ones who
know

how you like it   how you need
neither wife nor children now

Fais-nous confiance, they say,
trust us.

You will see
doctors, they will give you small
objects to swallow, each

at its designated time   in this way
your days will pass
                            We are the ones who know
better than doctors

who shuffle the deck, who can never
change the cards.

• • •

There is a man at the door
who wants you.

He is about to come in and he has already
entered.

He will always be there, about to come in, and he will
always have already been

inside.

His clothes are sharp, his face
taut.

He wants you
to pour him a Coke.

He wants you to join him, he needs you, you could
do things

together.

In the still of the night
in the clatter of the city

afternoon you are afraid
you wonder

who is this
he wants?

• • •

What would it be like if, crossing
a busy street, you didn't

bother to look
both ways?

If a driver slammed
on the brakes
                in time

you would go on.

If a driver didn't
slam on the brakes
                in time

you wouldn't go on

would there
be a difference

7. *Coeur*/Heart (1)

*Lacking close family ties in San Francisco, and
with his savings near depletion, Applicant has
found lodging with a series of roommates in the
city's small North African and Middle Eastern
communities. Because Applicant's outlook is
predominantly secular, his relationships with
more conservative Muslim immigrants have
been characterized by tension and suspicion
rather than mutual support. At the same time,
Applicant sometimes postpones calling his
family in Algeria so as not to reawaken painful
memories, or out of shame at his difficulty in
finding work in the city's depressed economy.*

Once, when she doesn't
hear from him,

Samira calls me. He's
OK, I tell her

carefully, I had
coffee with him just

the other day. I'll be sure to tell him
you called.

Mais qu'est-ce qui se passe, Ahmed?—it's later, I am trying not
    to
shout into the phone—

Ahmed, what's going on?

Then I remember, once, in a distant
city—far from my

children, my husband—how I hadn't
called them right away, how I had wanted

for a few
guarded moments to keep

impregnable
my fortress heart,

how I didn't want
to let down the gates

for fear
of what might enter
                    or escape.

Ahmed, I say—I am not shouting—Ahmed,
Samira needs you, the boys

do too, *Ils ont besoin
de votre force et de votre coeur,*
                              they need your

strength and
your heart.

Outside my kitchen it's
dark as I cross

this line
holding

both of us in

both of us
quiet now

a little longer

waiting
to hear what comes
                        then

Merci, he says, *merci*,
Judy you're right,
                he says,

merci.

8. *Coeur*/Heart (2)

> *The individual may not be able to recall with precision specific details of the [...] events but will be able to recall the major themes of the experiences.*

> (From *Examining Asylum Seekers*, Physicians for Human Rights)

When Ahmed gets
lost in the tangle of his

story, when he remembers how,
little by little, the fear

seeped into his life but can't summon
precisely or even

approximately those key
dates when the fear

edged closer,
            I try

to help him see, ask him to
choose from a set of colored felt-tips, to mark

each threat on a
sheet of white paper.

Let Call Number 1—a joke?—let it
be, he decides, the color of a sun still

half-shining. Let Call Number 2 be the blood
drying on his hands if he says yes.

Let the verses of the letter placed on the bar be
blue as the almost-heaven he is about

to lose, let his killers come by dark of night, their movements
marked in memory with a

thick, black pen.
        It's a Sunday afternoon at my office and we're making

our way—heads bent
above the paper—through

colors, through
points in time.

In eight days, at the Asylum Office, Ahmed
must tell his story to a

stranger who keeps the keys to all
he holds close, and buries

deep. Within that
forest, at this

moment we walk
together, try

to cross a fast-
moving stream
           and find

here a rock, solid and flat,
                     there an un-
steady, moss-slicked

stone beside a log that crumbles
instantly beneath

one
tentative step.

This is hard, he says, sometimes it all gets
jumbled up in my head.

I know, I say. It's really hard. Remember,
though, when the terrorists were

shooting you had no
choice but to run. Now

it's different, when you tell
your story it's where you stand
your ground, and strike back.
                    Votre histoire
c'est votre arme, I say, your story

is your weapon.

He tries again,
                and again
we move through the long

afternoon, over and
over till his story

enters his voice like a room where both can feel
at ease,
                till what he has lived

becomes at last
what he knows

how to speak.

He feels less nervous now, he says, and,
leaving, thanks me

for my help,
                Quand vous
parlez français, vous parlez

du fond de votre coeur. When you speak
French, he says, you speak

from the bottom of your heart.

It's as if he has turned,

suddenly, a key,

               something

is opening inside me, some
happiness welling

up, knowing
no bounds.

              Merci,

Ahmed, I say, thank you for
saying that,

             merci.

9. Accident

> *Within one year of the date of arrival in the U.S., an applicant must file an Asylum Application (USCIS Form I-589). An applicant will subsequently be interviewed at the appropriate Asylum Office by an Asylum Officer who has the authority to grant, but not to deny, asylum. If asylum is not granted, the applicant will receive a Notice to Appear before a judge of the Immigration Court. Waiting times for scheduled appearances before the Court typically range from several months to one or more years.*

He
is ready to tell his story.

She
is googling Algeria.

He
is having trouble remembering
the dates of his children's birthdays.

She
is having trouble believing
this man is a devoted father.

How many times, she wants to know, did he travel to Tunisia?
Did he ever apply for a U.S. visa while he was in Tunisia?

He is more confused than ever now, because sure, he used to go
there, weekends, when he was young, he and his friends would
pile into somebody's car after work and drive hard for a few
hours, hit one of the discos at the resorts just when the night was
heating up. Sundays, driving back, everyone was quieter, maybe a
little hung over but still, feeling pretty good—

what does Tunisia have to do with
his youngest son, waking,
crying his father's name?

Where is Tunisia
in the depths of night, when Ahmed is in San Francisco and his
    sons
are in Algeria?

She
is still googling Algeria. She knows

how to make the keys
chatter and race.

Finally she is ready to ask him, "Why
did you leave your country?"
                            Only now
he is not
entirely sure, he knows

it had something to do with
something bad that

happened there, something
he couldn't control, an

accident, he says, "I couldn't
stay, *J'ai eu un accident*, I had

an accident," these are
the words he uses, I hear them and

must speak them, "I had an accident," I say,
for him

who is slipping
is falling
        I

must follow I
am falling

down
to the bottom

of my heart.

10. Near the Courthouse

I am standing on Montgomery Street with a man I know
to be Berber but most would take to be
Arab and therefore

dangerous.

His eyes, though they are
by this time
              dear to me,
                           these eyes
at this moment
burn
       as if a great
horned owl had dropped
suddenly from some far sky
talons open
              above the curbside.

The hearing, for which we had prepared
eight months, did not go well.

Ahmed knows he should stop smoking but today he needs
a reason to look away

to follow the ashes flicked
to the curb   to pull in what's
left of his breath.

I am speaking with him as crowds rush past on Montgomery

the broker with his eyes
deep in his East Coast call,
                              the secretary squeezing
one too many errands into her break

I see them and I do not see them

the lawyers want me to tell Ahmed something he does not
want to hear

I am the messenger he shoots

to kill but I
am the one who fires back

                                        Ecoutez
I say

Listen

the lawyers are right and he has to
know

Ecoutez, Ahmed, écoutez
                              both of us

fierce
          in this second tongue
                              I am holding my own

11. Hearing

San Francisco
September 2009

He would always remember
how she turned to him,

how she looked over from
that high place where she

sat, suspended
in judgment—

while the prosecutor prodded and poked
at his life till Ahmed

flared up, his voice
scratching the courtroom's

hush
like a blade—

how he calmed himself quickly, just
as he'd practiced

with the attorneys, and
turning from his questioner

he spoke instead
to *Madame la Juge*,

          "Your Honor," he said, speaking

through the court interpreter,

                    "Excuse me, Your Honor, this
is difficult"—

how she was looking at him
as she listened, how he felt

her attention like someone stepping
out of a house to

meet him on a path, approaching—

"Yes," she said, "I
understand, Mr. Foudil.
                    You may

go on."

12. Epilogue

San Francisco
September 2011

*Asylum granted to Applicant by order of
the Immigration Court September 2009.
Derivative asylee status granted to wife and
two children subsequent to filing of three
USCIS Forms I-730. Family arrived in San
Francisco August 2011, where they joined Mr.
Foudil, currently employed as a custodian, in
his one-bedroom apartment.*

Those who have little now
give me everything

that first night, that first
sitting down

around their kitchen table, where those
I had known only

as photographs stapled into files
come

alive, stirring
around me they bustle and

tend to me, they feed me
chicken simmered with prunes,

they fold
softly at my throat

a scarf
the color of a darkening sea.

Samira is here now, and the
oldest boy, Hassan, and his

little brother, Aziz,
on whose head, after supper, Hassan

places, casually, his hand. Hassan
won't let his father smoke, he's

hidden Ahmed's cigarettes. Also,
Hassan tells him, "you've got to learn

English, man, you've already been here
five years."
                    But when they walk
with me across the city, so I can catch

my late train home, I stay
at the end

of our short procession,
talking

with Samira
while I half-watch

as father, as eldest son

bend their heads, each
to the other,

listening,
intent,
          then pull

apart, jostle
and laugh
                    they make

a way together
in the darkness

as winter's first
light rain

begins

Technical Note:
My Roles as Interpreter,
Translator, and Paralegal

During most of the period covered by these poems, I was em-
ployed as a senior paralegal in the San Francisco office of Orrick,
Herrington & Sutcliffe LLP, a large international law firm. In
connection with Orrick's extensive pro bono practice, I served as
a member of the Volunteer Interpreters Panel coordinated by the
Lawyers' Committee for Civil Rights of the San Francisco Bay
Area. Through the Panel I interpreted for asylum clients represented
by pro bono lawyers from other firms; I also served as an interpreter
and member of the legal team for clients represented by Orrick.

Working with attorneys and clients, I prepared and translated
written declarations, and helped develop and practice oral tes-
timony. I accompanied clients both to Asylum Office inter-
views (where I served as the interpreter) and to appearances in
Immigration Court, where I monitored the interpreting provided
by the court interpreter and explained uninterpreted proceedings
to the client during breaks.

My roles, then, made me what professional interpreters would
consider a hybrid: both paralegal and community interpreter/
translator. As the former, I served as a client advocate, doing what
was needed to build the strongest possible case for asylum. As the
latter, I was bound by intersecting but not always identical ethical
obligations that included accuracy and completeness but also
transparency and impartiality. The occasional tension between
these roles, played out over years in a variety of contexts, bit hard
and deep. The desire to explore it was one of the reasons I began
writing *Second Tongue*.

Acknowledgments

This is a short book with a long life behind it. For both, I owe thanks to many.

Elizabeth T. Gray, Jr.—poet, translator, lost-then-rediscovered friend—read *Second Tongue* in manuscript and chose portions ("Conduit" and "Consecutive") for *Epiphany*, whose editors shepherded them meticulously to publication. I will never forget the relief and joy I felt during my first phone call with Jonis Agee and Brent Spencer at Brighthorse Books, as I listened to their welcoming voices and realized my search for a publisher was over. To all these editors and publishers: my thanks.

At the heart of *Second Tongue* are four travelers whose journeys—ongoing as well as past—wipe clean the lens through which I look at what matters. The life I lead now follows in their steps.

My work with them was only one strand in a whole fabric of support, both individual and organizational. I am grateful to attorneys Rene Kathawala, Jim McQuade, Sarah Walcavich, Shaneeda Jaffer, Michelle Leung, Emilie Mathieu, Rocky Tsai, Bill Murray, and Mike Liever at Orrick, as well as to paralegal program director Selma Abdo and calendar and court services director David Swain; to attorneys Matt Kuykendall at Wilson Sonsini, Jayne Fleming at Reed Smith, Jeffrey Martins at Martins Law Office, and Christine Stouffer at Stouffer Law; and to psychologists Dr. Martine Aniel and Dr. Jeffrey Kaye.

The Lawyers' Committee for Civil Rights of the San Francisco Bay Area was and remains at the foundation of the work I describe in *Second Tongue*. LCCR coordinates, recruits, trains, inspires, cajoles, nudges, and otherwise maintains a small army of pro bono attorneys and interpreters, along with seasoned immigration attorney-mentors, to represent asylum seekers who otherwise could not afford counsel.

Survivors International (now part of the UC San Francisco-San Francisco General Hospital Trauma Recovery Center) provided clinical services that were critical in helping vulnerable clients endure the psychologically brutal process of revisiting and recounting the details of trauma in order to establish asylum claims. It was my privilege to interpret for one session between a client and SI's then-acting clinical director, Dr. Uwe Jacobs, whose wry humor, insight into the interpreter's role, and expertise on torture in its shifting, multi-tentacled shapes continue to enlighten and inspire me.

For invaluable strategic support and know-how, I am grateful to the Center for Gender and Refugee Studies at UC Hastings, San Francisco, and especially to Director Karen Musalo; to Berkeley's East Bay Sanctuary Covenant, especially Michael Smith, Refugee Rights Program Director; and to the New York office of Human Rights First, especially Deputy Legal Director Anwen Hughes.

From the first stirrings of these poems to their completion, Seth Schein has shared with me his astute intellect, magisterial scholarship, and warm support. To count him as a friend in my life has been both humbling and strengthening. Mardah Chami's belief in my writing— along with her humor, creative energy, and restless intelligence—have kept me steadily supplied with joy and surprises. As writers, readers, teachers, and stalwart friends, Bernard Gershenson and Paula Gocker have been, quite simply, essential.

I am grateful to each one of my French teachers, from seventh grade on, and for every minute of their patient, probing attention. But I owe special thanks to my Oberlin professor, the late Mathis Szykowski, whose pioneering course, "African Literature of French Expression," opened a door for me that, decades later, I walked through into another life. I am grateful to interpreter and translator David Sweet-Cordero at UC Berkeley Extension, for his teaching and thoughtful guidance. My thanks, as well, to poets and translators Jennifer Grotz and David Young, for their generous teaching, and for the gift of their poetry; and to pianist Betty Tipton, for teaching me, always and above all, to listen.

I have known Francine Fatoux since 1970, when we first taught at the Lycée Fénelon in Lille, France. In the years that followed, she became my model for what a friendship in two languages can be: complex, illuminating, regenerative. Sharing these poems aloud with her at my kitchen table was as important to me as any reading I have ever given.

To the friends, colleagues, and extended family who have listened, read, and encouraged, whether directly or indirectly—and whether listed individually here, or unnamed but always remembered— my gratitude runs strong.

Finally, without my immediate family this book, and the work it grew from, would have been inconceivable. My brother Fred Small has been, almost from the beginning, my companion in play, language, and song, and in the mysterious charges that reciprocally buzz between all three. His support for *Second Tongue* has been, at every stage, unstinting.

Neither of my parents is alive to read this book, yet both live in its pages. My father, Roger Small, showed me from childhood onward that advocacy takes many forms and can draw on a reticent tenderness as well as boldness. My mother, Ellen Small, read these poems with care and took their stories, like mine, deeply to heart. Whatever I know about permeable boundaries I first began learning as her young daughter. Her delight in savoring life's details and her unfaltering courage in bidding them goodbye sustain me now, each day and at every turn.

My son-in-law, Papa Assane Mbengue, and my daughter-in-law, April Zaat, have each in their distinctive ways enriched beyond measure my understanding of love, work, and family. Without them this book and its author would have been different, and circumscribed.

I have left until last the debts that lie the very closest to home. My son, Matthew Fitzgerald, has listened, prodded, and advised through the years of these poems' development, but in particular as they began to make their way to audiences. The tenacity, strategic clarity, and imagination he shows in his life strengthen and spark my own.

My daughter, Maura Fitzgerald, has been both reader and bulwark. Whether from New Orleans or South Africa, she shared her brilliant skills as a writer whenever I was most in need. She was always incisive. Always, almost instantly, there. Beyond the particulars of editing, her ability to see and deepen connections across borders, languages, cultures, and classes has informed every word of these poems.

My husband, Bob Fitzgerald, is my anchor, my wit-in-residence, beloved deflator and keeper-of-perspective. Long ago, in a dream, he showed me a room in our house that I had somehow overlooked, where I could write and be. Now, in our waking lives, *Second Tongue* is the book he helped make possible.

About the Author

JUDITH SMALL is a poet, educator, and member of the Volunteer Interpreters' Panel of the Lawyers' Committee for Civil Rights of the San Francisco Bay Area. Her writing has appeared in numerous magazines, including *The New Yorker*, *FIELD*, *Epiphany*, *Feminist Studies*, and *New Letters*. She has published one previous book, *From the Island* (Black Oyster), a mixed-genre memoir. Her prior awards include the CCLM Fels Award and two Pushcart Prize nominations. A finalist for the 2015 *FIELD* Poetry Prize, the 2015 Georgia Poetry Prize, and the 2016 Idaho Prize for Poetry, *Second Tongue* was the 2017 winner of the Brighthorse Prize in Poetry. Small coordinated the after-school Peer Interpreters Program at Oakland's Castlemont High School, where bilingual students from immigrant families learn the fundamentals of interpreting as they support newcomer students and their families.